Acknowledgements

The author would like to thank the following colle... family members for their help and support during production of this publication:

Eliza Johnson, Dahira Khalid, Sihao Zhou, Maciek Sarara and David and Erika Evans.

Mark Evans has been a teacher for over 25 years. He has taught in Australia, Japan, Malaysia and the UK. He graduated in languages from University College London and has a PGCE, CELTA, DELTA, Diploma in ESOL, as well as an MA in English Language Teaching. He currently lives in London where he teaches at a college and a university.

This edition published in London, England in 2018

ISBN-13: 978-1720541196 (CreateSpace-Assigned)
ISBN-10: 1720541191

Text copyright @2018, Mark Evans

No part of this book may be reproduced in any form, or by any means, without prior permission in writing from the author.

MeEducation

Please feel free to contact the author at - meeducation@yahoo.com

Visit the website at https://meeducation

Table of Contents

Adjectives 1	2
Adjectives 2	4
Adjectives 3	6
Adjectives 4	8
Adjective Exercise 1	10
Adjective Exercise 2	11
Adverbs 1	12
Adverbs 2	14
Adverbs 3	16
Adverb Exercise 1	18
Adverb Exercise 2	19
Useful Vocabulary 1	20
Useful Vocabulary 2	22
Useful Vocabulary 3	24
Useful Vocabulary 4	26
Review 1	28
Useful Vocabulary 5	29
Useful Vocabulary 6	31
Useful Vocabulary 7	33
Useful Vocabulary 8	35
Review 2	37
Useful Vocabulary 9	38
Useful Vocabulary 10	40
Useful Vocabulary 11	42
Useful Vocabulary 12	44
Review 3	46
Useful Vocabulary 13	47
Useful Vocabulary 14	49
Useful Vocabulary 15	51
Useful Vocabulary 16	53
Review 4	55
Useful Vocabulary 17	56
Useful Vocabulary 18	58
Useful Vocabulary 19	60
Useful Vocabulary 20	62
Review 5	64
Phobias	65
Answer Key	66

Adjectives 1

Match the adjectives with their definition:

	Rich
	Quiet, calm and worthy of respect
	Not smooth (esp. water)
	Has more than one meaning
	Speak honestly and not hide the truth
	Wet/sticky like a swamp
	Angry and ready to attack someone
	Doing something often and unable to stop
	Burning hot
	Very simple/basic
	Friendly
	Hard working in a careful way
	Acting in a confused way, lacking skill
	Harmful
	Spooky

---

affable   affluent   aggressive   ambiguous

blazing   boggy   bumbling   candid

choppy   compulsive   detrimental   dignified

diligent   eerie   elementary

Exercise

Insert the most appropriate adjective into the space below:

1) In the vacant tunnel there was an _____ silence.

2) The angry boxer was very _____.

3) Richmond is a very _____ area with many prosperous families.

4) The tempest made the waters of the loch very _____.

5) Delia was a _____ student and swotted every night.

6) Having only learnt French for two weeks, his oral skills were _____.

7) The funeral was a very _____ affair.

8) Smoking is very _____ to your health.

9) The _____ sun burnt his skin.

10) Reg was a _____ chap. He always made mistakes.

11) Never shying away from the truth, you could always expect _____ comments from the professor.

12) You could never work out what he meant; he was always _____.

Adjectives 2

Match the adjectives with their definition:

	Unlucky/unfortunate
	Keeps changing mind about what they want
	Remote/cut off
	Qualified/suitable to take part/receive
	People live there
	Deadly
	Unfriendly and aggressive
	Firm in friendship/support
	Too much/great
	Valid/acceptable
	Worthy of being respected/admired
	Shows good judgement/sense
	Attractive and tempting
	Clear and easy to understand
	Brave/fearless

eligible   enticing   excessive   fatal

fickle   hapless   honourable   hostile

inhabited   intrepid   isolated   judicious

legitimate   loyal   lucid

Exercise

Insert the most appropriate adjective into the space below:

1) In the Battle of Trafalgar, Nelson received a _____ wound from French gunfire.

2) Marco Polo was an _____ traveller.

3) The Government was urged to curb its _____ spending.

4) He was a very eloquent and _____ orator.

5) She was a _____ lass who always got herself into mischief.

6) Machu Picchu in Peru was _____ by the Incas.

7) The family cultivated an _____ farm far from any towns.

8) She found the aroma of fresh bread from the chic café _____.

9) Although he had fought for his country in the Falklands conflict, the council claimed he was not _____ for free housing.

10) Dave always changes his mind; he is very _____.

11) The cannibals on the island were very _____ to the mariners.

12) Britain and the USA are _____ allies.

Adjectives 3

Match the adjectives with their definition:

	Holy
	Not showing enough care and going wrong
	Continue for a long time without pause
	Positive about the future
	Need/depend on to be able to do something
	Not properly formed
	Makes you feel disgust
	Use a lot of effort, care and attention to detail
	Wanting material goods
	Gets angry quickly
	Makes you feel sadness/pity or lack of respect
	Slightly angry
	Closely connected with the subject
	Extremely unpleasant
	Unable to stay still/be happy where you are

---

malformed   materialistic   miffed   negligent

odious   optimistic   painstaking   pathetic

perpetual   quick-tempered   relevant   reliant

repugnant   restless   sacred

Exercise

Insert the most appropriate adjective into the space below:

1) As he was _____, Nigel decided to head down to the embankment and row his boat.

2) Time and space are _____.

3) Marjory was a _____ woman who got angry easily with her husband.

4) The bonsai tree was _____ and did not turn out the way they wanted it to.

5) The student was always _____ on her tutor for assistance.

6) She had just graduated from university with a first class honours degree and was _____ about the future.

7) Alan was very _____; he only cared about money.

8) No one liked him as he was an _____ man.

9) Jerusalem is _____ to many religions.

10) The train driver was found to be _____ as he fell asleep at the controls.

11) Leonardo Da Vinci painted the roof of the Sistine Chapel in _____ detail.

12) He read the book to get the _____ facts for the essay.

Adjectives 4

Match the adjectives with their definition:

	Has attractive scenery
	Extremely hot
	Something that has lost its firmness
	Pours down heavily and rapidly
	Do without other group members' agreement
	Encouraging resistance against government
	Unlike what people commonly expect
	Third in order/importance
	Watchful
	Agreement that is not definite/certain
	Wealthy
	Sits down a lot and does little exercise
	Nothing can alter/challenge it
	Strange, beautiful and impressive
	Very bad that you disapprove of

saggy   scenic   sedentary   seditious

tentative   tertiary   torrential   torrid

unassailable   unconventional   unilateral   vigilant

well-heeled   woeful   wondrous

Exercise

Insert the most appropriate adjective into the space below:

1) Where he lived next to the canal and bridge was rather _____.

2) Never one to follow a trend, Edward dressed in an _____ way.

3) The cyclist was so far ahead of the peloton that he was now in an _____ position.

4) Due to oil, Dubai is a _____ city in the Middle East.

5) Angkor Wat, in Cambodia, is truly a _____ spectacle.

6) Fred led a _____ lifestyle and became obese as a result.

7) The guardsman at the sentry box at the garrison remained _____ all night.

8) The _____ rain meant their progress was thwarted.

9) He wasn't sure if he could come, so he made a _____ agreement.

10) University is an example of _____ education.

11) Sid's mum was livid as his exam results were _____.

12) The heat in Death Valley, California is _____ with temperatures regularly exceeding forty degrees.

Adjective Exercise 1

Put the adjectives in the sentence to make them more interesting:

1) The man walked through the tunnel.

2) The path led to a forest.

3) A demon blocked the entrance to the citadel.

4) The bird flew over the rooftops.

5) There were many obstacles on the way to the city.

6) Cherry waited at her desk for the man to arrive.

7) The boy told his teacher that he had lost his homework.

8) The clouds raced across the sky like a jet plane.

9) A branch fell from the tree and hit a boy on his head.

10) The girl looked out of her window onto her garden.

Adjective Exercise 2

Put adjectives in the sentence to make them more interesting:

1) The car was in the river.

2) The clock was on the mantelshelf.

3) David left his friend's house in his mother's car.

4) The lady cooked Japanese food in the kitchen.

5) The girl watched a TV programme on her bed.

6) There was a picture on the wall in the living room.

7) The man waited for his dinner.

8) She drank a cup of coffee in the café.

9) They clambered over the rocks and saw a valley below.

10) The shed was at the back of the garden.

Adverbs 1

Match the adverbs with their definition:

	In a way that can't be measured
	Making you feel/remember something nice
	In an extremely bad way
	In a way related to money
	Persuade someone to do something kindly
	Morally correctly
	Different to usual in a bad way
	Not in a continuous way
	In a way that doesn't vary/change
	Showing great attention
	Usually, as a custom
	Confidently; definitely true
	Acting very excitedly/energetically
	In the past
	In a cold/empty way

---

abnormally   assuredly   bleakly   coaxingly

consistently   customarily   diabolically   ethically

evocatively   financially   formerly   frenetically

immeasurably   intently   intermittently

Exercise

Insert the most appropriate adverb into the space below:

1) You need to be _____ very well off to live in the new flats.

2) The EU was _____ called the EEC.

3) Although he was feeling under the weather, his mother looked at him _____ and said he would be fine tomorrow.

4) The size of the abscess on his leg was _____ large so he had to go to hospital.

5) They all listened to the erudite teacher _____.

6) She was a _____ good student throughout her school life; always getting 'A' grades.

7) He did _____ in all his exams; he did not pass any.

8) In the winter Iceland has a _____ beautiful landscape.

9) She dangled the string _____ in front of the kitten in an attempt to make her come out.

10) Due to power cuts, the lights came on _____.

11) People _____ exchange gifts at Christmas time.

12) They worked _____ to finish the project on time.

Adverbs 2

Match the adverbs with their definition:

	Jokingly
	Likely to cause death
	Beautifully and powerfully causing respect
	Possibly
	Youthfully, attractively and flexibly
	Always
	Strangely (in appearance or behaviour)
	Upsettingly
	Orderly and systematically
	Shockingly unusual and strange
	Angrily
	Threateningly
	Seemingly impossible as two facts oppose
	Impossible to prove wrong
	Lasting for a long time, difficult to eliminate

---

irascibly   irrefutably   kiddingly   kookily

lithely   majestically   menacingly   methodically

mortally   offensively   outrageously   paradoxically

perpetually   persistently   potentially

Exercise

Insert the most appropriate adverb into the space below:

1) The grand ship sailed _____ down the river.

2) Many people think that the sun will burn _____ but one day it will die.

3) The light-hearted doctor spoke to his child patients _____ to make them feel at ease.

4) Having been impaled, he was _____ wounded and died after an agonizing two days.

5) The students drank far too much port and behaved so _____ that they were barred from the pub.

6) The boxer stared at his bitter rival _____.

7) Drinking red wine is, _____, good for you.

8) The detective examined the crime scene _____, step by step for many hours before finding the evidence.

9) He didn't like the 'women only' sign and took it _____.

10) She had severe asthma and was coughing _____.

11) Working in a bank is _____ very lucrative.

12) The lawyer proved he was _____ guilty.

Adverbs 3

Match the adverbs with their definition:

	Morally correct
	Bravely
	Expressing criticism
	Behaving/dressing very formally/correctly
	Periodically
	Embarrassed as you know you did wrong
	Energetically/enthusiastically
	Comfortingly, to stop someone from worrying
	Not embarrassed/concealed
	Confusingly
	Strangely/unusually/remarkably
	Persuading people to oppose the government
	Appearing to ask a question
	Relating/involving only one side
	Happening irregularly for short periods

---

primly   puzzlingly   quizzically   reassuringly

reproachfully   righteously   seditiously   sheepishly

singularly   spasmodically   sporadically   unabashedly

unilaterally   valiantly   vivaciously

Exercise

Insert the most appropriate adverb into the space below:

1) The army fought _____ against the invaders and managed to protect their castle.

2) The commander accused his general of acting _____ and had him shot for treason.

3) He could not hide his feelings towards her. He was _____ in love and wanted the world to know it.

4) She _____ admitted to stealing from the shop.

5) Eliza dressed _____ for the formal event.

6) He had poor attendance and just came _____.

7) Mark looked at Paul _____ as if to ask for help.

8) Billie was confused and stared at her exam _____.

9) At her son's funeral she embraced her husband _____.

10) Hitler _____ broke his pact with Stalin and declared war.

11) After Ben's tutor saw his atrocious homework, he looked at him _____.

12) The young princess danced _____ to tempt him.

17

Adverb Exercise 1

Put adverbs in the sentence to make them more interesting:

1) She walked across the bridge which shook.

2) Eliza spoke to the student and the student wept.

3) He ran downstairs and asked for some food.

4) The lady sat down at the table and ate.

5) Lenny greeted everyone and turned on her computer.

6) Irene told her the news and Eli stood up.

7) The boy drank tea then went to his lesson.

8) He entered the derelict building and saw a ghoul staring at him.

9) Anna talked about her colleague then went back to work.

10) Mary walked out and slammed the door.

Adverb Exercise 1

Adverb Exercise 2

Put adverbs in the sentence to make them more interesting:

1) As the tempest approached, the boats rocked and the trees shook.

2) Adam sat down at the table and devoured his meagre rations.

3) Tina did her homework then went to bed.

4) Megan threw her bag on the floor and took out her make-up.

5) He gazed at the moon and prayed.

6) Shihao took the bus and talked with his friends.

7) They walked in the park then played on the swings and slides.

8) The sun rose in the east and shone all day.

9) They carved the pumpkin and put it outside the house.

10) David went to his room and played his piano.

Useful Vocabulary 1

Match the words with their definitions:

	Specially made for a customer
	Over-compliment someone
	Precious jewel/stone
	Beat repeatedly with fists
	Murder an important person
	Slight pause before you do something
	Well-expressed and persuasive
	Allow fresh air to enter
	Too satisfied and don't feel the need to worry
	Punishing
	Something that causes a lot of debate
	Irregular and changes a lot
	Escape
	Easily remembered phrase
	Spontaneous
	Do something special to remember an event
	Enter with difficulty
	Cautious/not confident of result
	Sad/worried feeling caused by something bad
	Severe tear in a pipe/body part
	Deceitful action

---

assassinate   bespoke   commemorate   complacent
controversy   dismay   eloquent   flatter
flee   fluctuate   gem   hesitate
impromptu   penetrate   pummel   punitive
rupture   ruse   slogan   tentatively   ventilate

Exercise

Put the new words into the gaps in the correct grammatical form:

1) As they sailed along, water was unable to _____ the boat.

2) Like all commodities, the price of oil _____ every day.

3) Being a great orator, he gave a very _____ speech.

4) The felon _____ President Kennedy in Dallas, 1963.

5) Salvaging what they could, the civilians _____ the bombardment of their town before it was obliterated.

6) Helen _____ slightly before she blissfully accepted the marriage proposal.

7) The prosperous businessman ordered a _____ suit from the tailor in Savile Row.

8) They allotted a lot of time to make a new advertising _____.

9) His brother made an _____ visit to his opulent mansion.

10) As a result of the car accident, he _____ his internal organs.

11) The dead of the two world wars are _____ every November in a poignant ceremony.

12) Lama meticulously placed the tiny _____ into the gold ring.

13) John told his family he was destitute and lived in a hovel but it was all a _____ to get money out of them.

14) Phil _____ put his foot on the bridge over the ravine to test it.

15) Jade opened the windows to _____ the room as it was rather musty and full of mildew.

Useful Vocabulary 2

Match the words with their definitions:

	Strong, pleasant smell
	A young person training on the job
	A big rounded rock
	Gather together in a group
	A business or company
	Can't be broken into
	Think carefully for a while
	A confusing or difficult problem
	A lot of noise, confusion and excitement
	Dark and dirty with poor visibility
	Something expressed indirectly
	Acting dishonestly to get what you want
	Disgusting, very unpleasant
	Speaking loudly to get your ideas across
	Irrational fear/hated of something
	Allow other beliefs/ideas
	Large, flat, high area of land
	Done suddenly without planning
	Slightly open
	Beg
	Free someone

abominable   ajar   apprentice   aroma
boulder   commotion   congregate   conundrum
enterprise   implicit   impregnable   liberate
murky   phobia   plateau   plead
ponder   spontaneous   tolerant   unscrupulous   vociferous

Exercise

Put the new words into the gaps in the correct grammatical form:

1) A massive _____ fell down the hill and into the choppy river.

2) As the grubby door was _____, he peered in to the peasant's hovel.

3) Due to their fortifications, their castle was totally _____.

4) The beggar skulked around the town _____ for help.

5) Billy joined the factory as a young _____ as he wanted to pursue a career in manufacturing.

6) After Rome was _____ from Nazi occupation, the mayhem finally ceased.

7) The water in the lagoon was _____ making it hard to see.

8) His _____ of spiders made him quiver.

9) There was a piquant _____ of Thai food coming from the chic new restaurant.

10) Steve was a _____ opponent of the fiasco.

11) The raucous barbarians _____ at the gates of the city.

12) As the orator stepped down, _____ applause broke out.

13) She was posed with the _____ of what to salvage from the debris of her home.

14) Lucy was very _____ and open to new ideas.

15) With the inhospitable blizzard raging outside, Scott _____ what he should do.

23

Useful Vocabulary 3

Match the words with their definitions:

	Completely wet
	Wave a weapon in display
	Kept imprisoned/enclosed
	Encourage someone to take action
	Slope at a certain angle
	Great praise and admiration
	Succeed in getting something back
	Complete/pure
	People you are descended from
	Elaborate/has a lot of decoration
	Fight
	Straps around a horse's head and mouth
	Speak in a brief, rude way
	Feeling dizzy looking down from a great height
	Strange and hard to explain
	Inactive now but active later
	Not important/interesting
	Dislike someone/something as it's beneath you
	Cord in body that joins muscle to bone
	People/animals that live in a place
	Extremely painful

adulation   ancestor   brandish   brawl
bridle   captive   contempt   curt
dormant   embolden   excruciating   incline
inhabitant   ornate   retrieve   sheer
sodden   tendon   trivial   uncanny   vertigo

Exercise

Put the new words into the gaps in the correct grammatical form:

1) Looking down was harrowing as he suffered from _____.

2) After the earthquake, many _____ decided to flee.

3) The king relished the _____ that he received from his people.

4) Craftsmen had carved very _____ designs on the door.

5) The horse cantered as the knight _____ a fearsome lance.

6) She had to climb a steep _____ as the residence was at the top of the hill.

7) Josh loathes his boss and treats him with utter_____.

8) Having been maimed by flying shrapnel, he found the pain _____.

9) Many of my _____ emigrated to Rhodesia in the last century.

10) In World War I, the boots of the British soldiers became _____ as the trenches were full of water.

11) Mary put the _____ on the horse.

12) As he had run so far, his _____ gave him excruciating pain.

13) After drinking too much in the alehouse, the raucous apprentices began to _____ in the street.

14) They were held _____ in the dank prison cell and only had stagnant water to quench their thirst.

15) The hedgehog was _____ deep in the undergrowth awaiting the end of winter.

Useful Vocabulary 4

Match the words with their definitions:

	Violent, windy storm
	Munch
	Pay great attention to detail
	Trick to lead/send someone to the wrong place
	Enough of something
	Famous for being bad
	Joy often caused by someone's misfortune
	State of confusion and chaos
	Market with stalls, especially in Middle East
	Adult male horse
	Read/look through in a casual way
	Get off a ship/plane
	Unexpected difficulty
	Meat eater
	Get something when someone dies
	Gradually remove/destroy
	Young person
	Smaller-sized newspaper
	Put yourself in someone's shoes emotionally
	Funny/amusing way of behaving/moving
	Craze

---

ample   antics   bazaar   browse
carnivore   chomp   decoy   disembark
empathy   erode   fad   fastidious
glee   infamous   inherit   juvenile
pandemonium   snag   stallion   tabloid   tempest

Exercise

Put the new words into the gaps in the correct grammatical form:

1) There was a violent _____ brewing on the scenic loch.

2) There was _____ room to manoeuvre the car on the steep incline.

3) The intrepid travellers _____ from the ferry onto the boggy terrain.

4) She _____ through the wondrous book at a leisurely pace.

5) As his opponents faltered, he looked at them with _____.

6) Lions are _____; they forage for meat.

7) Hordes of _____ were involved in the commotion outside the disco.

8) The panda _____ away at the bamboo in the lush forest.

9) She was a _____ person with great attention to detail.

10) When his erudite grandmother died he _____ a fortune.

11) The cliff started to _____ due to the wind.

12) Eliza had a lot of _____ for John as she had been in the same situation herself.

13) Breakdancing was a _____ in the 1980s and many juveniles had impromptu dance competitions.

14) She bought an antique amulet in the _____.

15) The Daily Mail is an example of a _____ newspaper.

Review 1 *(use the vocabulary from 1-4)*

Across
2. dizzy from heights
5. fight
6. enough
8. smell
9. escape
11. enter
15. think
16. let air flow
19. sleeping

Down
1. fear
3. jewel
4. get back
5. rock
7. eat
10. craze
12. storm
13. problem
14. trick
17. unimportant
18. slightly open

28

Useful Vocabulary 5

Match the words with their definitions:

	Large in size/weight
	Be most powerful/important
	Think a lot (negatively)
	Silly/careless (spoken) mistake
	Don't include/leave out something
	Bring in goods from another country
	Sing/play music on the street for money
	Examine very carefully
	Persuade someone to do something
	Study very hard (especially for an exam)
	Someone who is extremely wicked/cruel
	Strong, sudden rush of wind
	Ability to hold/contain something
	Concert hall
	Someone who doubts what others believe
	Understood but not said directly
	Gather/collect
	Loan from bank to buy a house
	Hard (usually physical) work; workers
	Good/useful qualities of something
	Lower part of place/thing

accumulate   auditorium   brood   busk
capacity   dominate   entice   fiend
gaffe   gust   hefty   import
labour   merit   mortgage   nether
omit   sceptic   scrutinize   swot   tacit

29

Exercise

Put the new words into the gaps in the correct grammatical form:

1) He had to take out a huge _____ to be able to purchase his rural residence with its very own lake.

2) As a result of the blizzard, snow _____ on the stark landscape.

3) When people spell 'misspell', they often _____ the second 's'.

4) When the detective received the evidence, he _____ every detail, judiciously.

5) As he had an exam the next day, he had to _____ up on all the material.

6) They play a wide genre of concerts in the _____.

7) The Prime Minister made a huge _____ when he erroneously insulted the ambassador.

8) He carried a _____ pile of scintillating books.

9) Sweden _____ most of its crude oil from Saudi Arabia.

10) After losing the bet, he became petulant and went to his bedroom to _____.

11) Genghis Khan _____ central Asia with his nomadic warriors.

12) A huge _____ of wind blew the pier down into the sea causing mayhem.

13) He earned money _____ in the streets with a guitar he had salvaged.

14) The _____ of the auditorium was three hundred people.

15) Coal mining is considered hard _____.

Useful Vocabulary 6

Match the words with their definitions:

	Connected with sea/ships/sailing
	Catch and arrest someone
	Something lucky that happens by accident
	Say you publicly support someone/something
	Store room/cupboard for food
	Money available and a plan how to spend it
	Greatly impress someone with beauty/brains
	Collect and keep large amounts of things
	The art/practice of cooking/eating good food
	Solemn promise
	Noise of people clapping to show appreciation
	Person/animal that eats flesh of its own type
	Managing relations between two countries
	Ruin and destroy
	Persuade/influence someone to do something
	Destroy slowly, especially with chemicals
	Feeling sick and wanting to vomit
	Small articles of various sizes
	Enjoy oneself, showing low (moral) standards
	Make completely wet; fill completely
	Talk/say quickly making it hard to understand

---

applause   apprehend   bedazzle   budget
cannibal   corrode   decadent   diplomacy
endorse   fluke   gastronomy   hoard
induce   jabber   larder   marine
nausea   oath   paraphernalia   ravage   saturate

Exercise

Put the new words into the gaps in the correct grammatical form:

1) The barren landscape had been _____ by famine and floods.

2) The police _____ the infamous fugitive.

3) As drought loomed, the civilians _____ ample supplies of water.

4) The flamboyant businessman led a _____ lifestyle and neglected his company.

5) When the composer arrived he was greeted with great _____.

6) The golfer's hole in one was a complete _____.

7) The accountants gathered to discuss the _____ for the organisation.

8) The peasant lady was _____ by the charming aristocrat.

9) He made an _____ that he would never drink again.

10) As David had left the batteries in his toy for so long, they became _____ and had to be disposed of.

11) Good _____ between countries is extremely important to avoid war.

12) The athlete _____ the product and earned a lot of money.

13) When the seafarers landed on the desert island they were petrified to find out that there were _____ lurking in the darkness.

14) Before fridges, provisions were kept in the _____.

15) On the long sea voyage, the mariner became overwhelmed by _____, especially when it became choppy.

Useful Vocabulary 7

Match the words with their definitions:

	System where private people control property
	Animals of a particular area
	Large knife with a broad blade
	Subtract from the total
	Moves further back into the distance
	Jaw bone of an animal, fish or bird
	A person's child/children
	Fail to look after properly
	Buy/get something
	Walk in a casual, unhurried way
	Someone who sells objects house to house
	Greater amount of something than you need
	People of high birth and high social status
	Three times
	Someone who lives frugally away from society
	Come out from an enclosed space
	Defender of a way of life
	Cut skin badly and deeply
	Neutral, unbiased
	Junior officer in army, navy or air force
	Argue about a small matter

```
acquire      bastion      capitalism    deduct
emerge       fauna        gentry        hermit
impartial    lacerate     lieutenant    machete
mandible     neglect      offspring     pedlar
plethora     quibble      recede        saunter     thrice
```

Exercise

Put the new words into the gaps in the correct grammatical form:

1) As it was a beautiful day, Wade _____ on down the country lanes.

2) Referees have a duty to be _____.

3) The Galapagos Islands have unique flora and _____.

4) He was a _____ in the Royal Air Force.

5) Money was _____ from the waiter's wages for being so reckless.

6) Roger was scolded by his mother as he _____ to feed his cat.

7) _____ is the direct opposite of communism.

8) When the sea _____ he knew that there was going to be a huge tsunami.

9) She used a _____ to cut down the sugar cane.

10) He _____ his fortune from his affluent mother.

11) There is a _____ of flora and fauna in the Amazon rain forest.

12) The fox _____ from the undergrowth where it had been lurking.

13) His _____ had all moved home and he was now alone.

14) A _____ resided on the isolated peninsula.

15) Sophia _____ with the waiter as the bill was excessive.

Useful Vocabulary 8

Match the words with their definitions:

	View where you can see far and wide
	Armed robber in lawless land
	Man who behaves aggressively/impolitely
	Ability to understand something after the event
	Refuse to obey
	Cover in a thin layer of gold
	Group of most powerful/rich/talented
	Someone who is new/inexperienced
	Small (useless) objects people enjoy looking at
	Treat someone (physically) roughly
	Long story from medieval times
	Joking/teasing talk amongst friends
	Express an opinion
	Edge/verge of something important/terrible
	Plants growing in a particular area
	Having no energy/interest
	System where no one obeys rules/laws
	Violent slaughter of many people, esp. in war
	Start burning/explode
	Object from past which is still used
	Fortress/stronghold in/near a city

anarchy	bandit	banter	brink
carnage	citadel	defy	elite
flora	gild	hindsight	ignite
knick-knacks	languor	lout	manhandle
novice	opine	panorama	relic	saga

Exercise

Put the new words into the gaps in the correct grammatical form:

1) From Clifton Suspension Bridge you can get a fantastic _____ of the surrounding gorge.

2) There is a wide array of _____ and fauna in Cape Town.

3) _____ used to roam the Wild West robbing stagecoaches.

4) The inhabitants retreated to the _____ in times of war.

5) If you go to Oxford, you are considered _____.

6) When the civil war took hold in Somalia there was complete _____.

7) The friends were in a good mood and exchanged _____ in the bistro.

8) The old professor's house was cluttered with many _____.

9) The bandits lit a match which _____ the fuse to blow up the safe.

10) There was a bunch of drunken _____ fighting by the harbour.

11) The passenger refused to pay for his ticket, so he was _____ off the train.

12) The company had suffered huge losses and was on the _____ of disaster.

13) The museum had many _____ from the Victorian era.

14) As a result of bombarding the citadel there was complete _____, with many casualties.

15) The Vikings were famous for writing many _____.

Review 2 *(use the vocabulary from 5-8)*

Across
2. no laws
4. clap
5. worker
7. sing for money
9. flowers
11. minus
13. good point
14. three times
17. error
18. sea
19. the best

Down
1. long story
3. animals
6. children
7. spending plan
8. joke
10. promise
12. leave out
15. lucky
16. live alone

37

Useful Vocabulary 9

Match the words with their definitions:

	Walk slowly in a relaxed manner
	Item of clothing
	Second most important person in organisation
	Cross breed
	Large quantity of food/drink
	Body of a dead animal
	Take something away as punishment
	Disagree in a scornful, mocking way
	Liberate
	Gaffe/socially embarrassing action/mistake
	Have great longing/desire for something
	Attack someone violently
	State of being totally unaware/unconscious
	Signal with hand for someone to come closer
	System where the ruler is always female
	In case
	Reminds you of something
	Physical strength
	Things/ideas are similar/related
	Rude/wrong behaviour
	Repeatedly and gently beat a surface

---

amble   assail   beckon   brawn
carcass   confiscate   deputy   emancipate
faux pas   garment   hanker   hybrid
improper   kindred   lashings   lest
matriarchy   oblivion   patter   redolent   scoff

Exercise

Put the new words into the gaps in the correct grammatical form:

1) The picture was _____ of a wealthy country garden.

2) Rain _____ intermittently on the window pane.

3) The Prime Minister did not know how to behave at the ambassadorial event and made a _____.

4) They _____ reticently across the pasture to the haven.

5) Lucy's behaviour at the party was most _____.

6) Due to her qualifications, she became the _____ head of the school.

7) Grandad always _____ about going back to Ireland.

8) The erudite old man _____ the boy to come closer.

9) Maimed by the attack, he passed out and drifted into _____.

10) As David wouldn't stop playing his computer game, his father decided to _____ it.

11) William Wilberforce was on a mission to _____ all slaves.

12) The plant is a _____ of two different species.

13) Cherry killed the robin and all that was left was its half-eaten _____.

14) The jumble sale was selling a wide variety of _____.

15) He loved his English breakfast served with _____ of bacon.

Useful Vocabulary 10

Match the words with their definitions:

	Narrow valley with steep sides
	Understand someone's feelings/situation
	Next/close to something, esp. different
	God/goddess
	Group of people/ideas most people belong to
	Opinion/belief about a particular subject
	Saying that expresses a general truth
	Probability
	Noisy and disorderly incident/commotion
	Heavy sword with a (usually) curved blade
	Line of objects to stop people getting past
	Peaceful/happy time from the past
	Quality/ability you are born with
	Long, exciting, eventful journey
	Noisy argument/disagreement
	Treatment for illness without drugs/operations
	Emptiness/vacuum
	Level of ability and intelligence
	Story intended to teach moral lesson
	Harvest
	Formal agreement b/t people or governments

```
adage       altercation    barricade    calibre
  deity       empathize      fable       gorge
halcyon       innate        juxtapose   kerfuffle
likelihood   mainstream      notion      odyssey
  pact         reap          sabre       therapy    void
```

Exercise

Put the new words into the gaps in the correct grammatical form:

1) A great bridge spanned the _____.

2) The old man looked back at his _____ days with a smile.

3) The company hired the candidate that they thought had the highest _____.

4) He returned from his _____ after travelling for many years.

5) The Greeks were famous for writing many _____.

6) There is an old _____ that says that time is the great healer.

7) The soldier drew his _____ and charged at his foe.

8) Florence Nightingale was a kind nurse who was able to _____ with her patients.

9) Germany and the Soviet Union made a _____ never to go to war with each other.

10) A black hole is a _____ into which no one has ever entered.

11) The two men were arrested after an _____ outside the tavern.

12) In the dying days of World War Two the Germans erected _____ in the streets to thwart the advancing Russian forces.

13) After sowing many seeds, he _____ the harvest in autumn.

14) Learning how to walk is _____ in all humans.

15) After suffering such mental anguish, he decided to seek _____ for his condition.

Useful Vocabulary 11

Match the words with their definitions:

	Feeling of comfort that makes you less sad
	Long, angry, criticizing speech
	Waste foolishly
	Someone who knows a lot about a subject
	A way of considering something/a viewpoint
	Very serious; very bad
	Someone involved in an activity for a long time
	Search for something (esp. food)
	Annoy, trouble and frustrate someone
	Special right/privilege given to someone
	Respectful behaviour
	Cannot see far away things
	Two or more people fully in agreement
	Slope/curve gently
	Facilities for people's convenience
	Rarely
	Offended/ashamed/embarrassed
	Solemn promise
	Know someone very well/closely
	Happens at the beginning of a process
	Thick and sticky (liquid)

amenity   concession   connoisseur   dire
forage   initial   intimate   myopic
mortified perspective   pledge   reverent
seldom   solace   squander   tirade
unanimous undulate   veteran   viscous   vex

Exercise

Put the new words into the gaps in the correct grammatical form:

1) Discounted admission fees to the gardens are a _____ that some O.A.P.s may have.

2) When he realised that he had lost such a large sum of money, he was _____.

3) Parks, libraries and a new leisure centre are just a few of the _____ that the new town has.

4) Now that he was an adult, he could view the situation from a different _____.

5) He knows a lot about food and is considered as a _____ by all who know him.

6) He required glasses as he became _____.

7) Mel _____ all his money and was broke.

8) The jury reached a _____ verdict that Mr Johnson was innocent.

9) The rolling hills _____ into the distance.

10) The dogs _____ for truffles in the undergrowth.

11) She _____ to assist the victims of the terrible tragedy.

12) After being made redundant from the steel works, his financial situation became _____.

13) They were close friends and had a very _____ relationship.

14) Simon was a _____ of the Falklands War.

15) His depression led him to seek _____ in alcohol.

Useful Vocabulary 12

Match the words with their definitions:

	Particular type of land
	Spend a lot of money
	Calm and peaceful
	Something that causes a lot of harm/suffering
	Wasting money carelessly
	Completely lacking in something
	Make something stretch tight
	Behaving in a proud unfriendly way
	Honest and morally correct behaviour
	Set of beliefs of a religion/system
	Looks cheap and badly made
	Not being serious when you should be
	Stay in a place that is not home for a short time
	Action/event different to what is usual
	Be offended by someone
	Make you feel annoyed
	Official leaders of religious activity
	Possibility that something will happen
	Behaving in an irregular way
	Control/limit something harmful
	Walk slowly and reluctantly

---

aberration   clergy   curb   devoid
doctrine   erratic   frivolous   haughty
irk   profligate   prospect   rectitude
scourge   serene   sojourn   splurge
tacky   tauten   terrain   traipse   umbrage

Exercise

Put the new words into the gaps in the correct grammatical form:

1) After winning on the horses he _____ out on a luxury cruise.

2) The crying baby _____ him immensely.

3) The _____ of Iceland tends to be rocky and barren.

4) With a heavy rucksack, they had to _____ across the whole town.

5) He bought cheap furniture which made his room look very _____.

6) Jeff took _____ at the rude remark.

7) Many members of the _____ reside in the Vatican.

8) Gordon was very _____ with other people's money.

9) With only meagre rations left, the fur trappers had little _____ of surviving the winter.

10) He just didn't care; he was totally _____ of any compassion.

11) Mark _____ in Malaysia for six weeks when he was younger.

12) Dave's father felt totally _____ relaxing in his tranquil garden.

13) As Don had been drinking, his driving was _____ and he was apprehended by the police.

14) He had to _____ the ropes of the sailing vessel.

15) Locusts are a great _____ in Africa as they can eat crops, which may lead to famine.

45

Review 3 *(use the vocabulary from 9-12)*

Across
4. live
6. in case
7. liberate
9. rarely
12. search
13. clothes
14. long journey
16. saying
18. strength
19. annoy

Down
1. empty
2. first
3. respectful
5. call
8. religious leader
9. waste
10. ground
11. god
15. agreement
17. irregular

Useful Vocabulary 13

Match the words with their definitions:

	Structure in water used to get on/off boats
	Place where someone lives
	Number; finger
	Feeling of hate
	Guess possible answers
	Move heavy object using great effort
	Cause someone to be angry
	Move/fall suddenly and deeply
	Move slowly/stand in public without reason
	Pattern or design
	Has a pleasant smell
	Climb up and across
	Fat
	Cover/surround something completely
	Very surprising in a pleasing way
	Too eager to instruct others
	Large number of people/things
	Behaving wrongly
	Seems to be right but is wrong
	Fixed, limited amount
	Small, dry bits that burn easily

abode   aromatic   clamber   digit enmity   enrage   envelop   errant heave   jetty   loiter   motif multitude   officious   plump   plunge quota   specious   speculate   stupendous   tinder

47

Exercise

Put the new words into the gaps in the correct grammatical form:

1) He _____ into the river below for a swim.

2) As she had been devouring ice cream all summer, she was beginning to become rather _____.

3) Plumes of smoke _____ the whole building.

4) The boat was waiting at the _____ ready to ferry the weary travellers across the murky loch.

5) There was a pleasant smell in the conservatory from all of the _____ herbs.

6) The hermit lived in a humble _____ atop a bleak hillside.

7) Ralph _____ over the rocks and plunged into the lagoon.

8) A small crowd of juveniles were _____ outside on the bench.

9) Simon was _____ when he found out his best friend had betrayed him.

10) He looked around for _____ to help light the camp fire.

11) Ancient Britons had to _____ huge slabs of rock in order to construct Stonehenge.

12) Rationing meant you were only allowed a small _____ of fresh meat.

13) Winning first prize was a _____ result.

14) He was a very _____ man who took his job far too seriously.

15) As they weren't sure, they could only _____ as to the reasons for the crash.

48

Useful Vocabulary 14

Match the words with their definitions:

	Drain, gutter
	Layer that covers something
	Dirt ingrained on a surface
	Break into many pieces
	Short hairs on a man's chin
	Sudden increase in quantity of something
	Big claw of a bird of prey
	Wild thorny blackberry bush
	Heavy rain in a short time
	Fall in large quantities, hanging; waterfall group
	Burn with hot water
	Flow of cool air into a room
	Make air in the stomach come to the mouth
	Very bright/intense
	Large deep cooking pot
	Creep about, esp. animals hunting
	Tiny yellow/green plant growing on rocks/walls
	Chew repeatedly, usually destroying it
	Fixed cover for shelter/decoration
	Move quickly/suddenly
	Stately/grand

---

belch   brambles   canopy   cascade
cauldron   dart   downpour   draught
gnaw   grime   gully   lichen
majestic   prowl   scald   shatter
shroud   stubble   surge   talon   vivid

Exercise

Put the new words into the gaps in the correct grammatical form:

1) As it was damp, _____ grew on the walls of the castle.

2) Water from the heavy _____ penetrated the roof of the derelict building and the floor was now sodden.

3) After the meal, the juvenile _____ loudly.

4) The hare _____ across the meadow as the farmer approached.

5) She cut herself as she clambered over the _____ by the brook.

6) Lions are nocturnal, _____ at night in the savannah.

7) The water _____ down the rugged mountainside.

8) The eagle's _____ was as sharp as a razor.

9) The _____ made the pauper's hovel particularly cold in winter.

10) Clouds _____ Mount Fuji in the summer months.

11) Rodger neglected to listen to his mother's advice and was _____ by boiling water.

12) Rats like to _____ on cables making them hazardous.

13) The crystal decanter _____ as it hit the floor.

14) As he spontaneously decided to do out, Dave had no time to shave his _____.

15) She had a _____ dream about living on a tropical island with stupendous views of an enchanted lagoon.

Useful Vocabulary 15

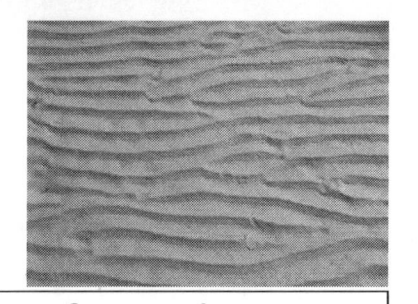

Match the words with their definitions:

	Deep line/fold in the surface of something
	Someone who behaves in a different way
	Regular beat felt from the heart
	Face/expression
	Hold/put something in a balanced position
	Hit someone/something many times
	Skin on top of the head
	Breathe suddenly in a way that can be heard
	Twist face unpleasantly showing pain/dislike
	Become marked with a line by folding/wrinkling
	Make it difficult for someone to do something
	Expect
	Homeless person
	Unable to feel anything
	Look at someone in an unpleasant way
	Wind/twist into rings
	Awake but behaving like asleep
	The way someone behaves/speaks/dresses
	Speak/smile in an unkind disrespectful way
	Long deep cut
	Makes you feel something is evil

anticipate	batter	coil	countenance
crease	demeanour	eccentric	furrow
gash	gasp	grimace	hamper
leer	numb	poise	pulse
scalp	sinister	sneer	tramp	trance

Exercise

Put the new words into the gaps in the correct grammatical form:

1) Trevor Bayliss, an _____ inventor who invented the wind up radio, lived on an island in the middle of the Thames.

2) There were scores of people eagerly _____ the visit by the royal family.

3) His commute to work was _____ by the train strike.

4) As the ballerina collapsed, all the audience _____.

5) The torrential rain _____ down on the thatched roof.

6) Kate's fingers were _____ as a corollary of the sub-zero temperatures.

7) Ken needed to iron his shirt as it had a _____ in.

8) Having just woken up, he looked like he was in a deep _____.

9) The old man had deep _____ on his forehead.

10) He _____ when he saw the carcass which had been devoured by the fox.

11) He had a massive _____ after being cut with a sword.

12) They thought he was dead but the paramedic could detect a faint _____.

13) Her _____ was encrusted with thick dandruff.

14) The evil dictator looked at him with a _____ expression.

15) Diana frequently helped _____ to find new homes.

Useful Vocabulary 16

Match the words with their definitions:

	Walk with difficulty due to bad leg/foot
	Very thin from illness/hunger
	Gentle and quiet, unwilling to argue
	Lonely and unhappy
	Have a strong bad smell
	Behaving secretively
	Sudden uncontrollable movement in face
	Flow thickly and slowly out of something
	Crush to make smaller and bent
	Fat, round and unattractive
	Open contempt
	Twist from normal shape to make unattractive
	Bunch of hair close together
	Behaving in an anxious/excited way
	Sharp curved point of a hook
	Small thick mass of grass
	Burn a surface slightly
	Anger and hatred
	Let saliva drip out of mouth
	Move quickly and timidly
	Flat areas on forehead

barb	bile	bulbous	contort
crumple	emaciated	forlorn	furtive
hobble	manic	meek	ooze
reek	scorn	scuttle	singe
slobber	temples	tic	tuft	tussock

Exercise

Put the new words into the gaps in the correct grammatical form:

1) Patricia dislocated her ankle and slowly _____ off down the long path to the hospital.

2) He had _____ eyes which were as big as balloons.

3) After finding out the evil truth, she screamed with absolute _____.

4) She was a _____ girl who never argued with anyone.

5) Ed had a _____ expression on his face from the agonizing pain.

6) When he turned on the light he could hear the cockroaches _____ away.

7) Living alone in the near-deserted village, she felt _____ after the loss of her best friend.

8) Denise leaned over the candle and accidentally _____ her hair.

9) In a petulant mood, he _____ the letter and threw it in the bin.

10) When he woke up he had a _____ of hair protruding.

11) The soldier cut himself on the _____ in the wire.

12) After three years of barely surviving in the ice, he was finally discovered in an _____ condition.

13) As the creature lay slain in its lair, gunge _____ out of its fatal wounds.

14) Immense pain emanated from his _____.

15) When we drove past the abattoir it _____ of dead animals.

Review 4 *(use the vocabulary from 13 - 16)*

Across
3. residence
5. beat
6. big cut
8. limit
9. clumped hair
10. number
12. stink
13. cover
14. bright
15. expect
17. hang around
18. make angry

Down
1. anger and hatred
2. twist
4. cold wind
6. eat
7. dribble
9. homeless
11. dirt
16. heartbeat

Useful Vocabulary 17

Match the words with their definitions:

	Stick out from somewhere
	Unpleasant, sticky substance
	Very cruel and violent
	Holding non-standard religious views
	Exaggeration
	Words/expressions used by a particular group
	Lack of order
	Full of self-importance and too serious
	Mixture of things not usually together
	Written statement of beliefs by political party
	Read quickly to get gist
	Exciting/desirable quality
	Steal things of little value
	Not firm/soft and fat
	Read carefully in a formal manner
	Subjects taught by a school/college
	Angry and silent believing you were wronged
	Main idea of what someone has said/written
	Cause a lot of damage/problems
	Produce a smell/light
	Has no colour or decoration

allure   brutal   curriculum   emanate
flabby   gist   gunge   havoc
hyperbole   jargon   manifesto   pagan
pompous   potpourri   peruse   pilfer
protrude   skim   stark   sullen   wreak

Exercise

Put the new words into the gaps in the correct grammatical form:

1) The boat cruised along the river past a _____ of buildings.

2) He was a petty criminal who often used to _____ from shops.

3) Parched, he could not resist the _____ of the oasis shimmering in the distance.

4) He perused the report to get a _____ of what was written.

5) Accountants and bankers use a great deal of _____ so not everyone can understand them.

6) The pupils study a plethora of subjects on the _____ at school.

7) When he opened the fridge there was green _____ oozing from the containers.

8) All the political parties release their _____ before the general election.

9) There was a peculiar light _____ from the swamp.

10) Sue _____ the brochure to get the gist.

11) There was a large abscess which _____ from his leg.

12) As he hadn't trained for a long time, his stomach became rather _____.

13) The storm wreaked enormous _____ on the Caribbean island.

14) After the shelling in World War One the landscape was _____; not a single tree was left standing.

15) She was a _____ widow who refused to talk to anyone.

57

Useful Vocabulary 18

Match the words with their definitions:

	Outside edge
	Believable
	Make stronger with additions
	Statement of truth with two opposite sides
	Great change and confusion
	Confuse
	Chains for a prisoner's foot to prevent escape
	Give one's name to something/a place/tribe
	Enough/good enough
	Sorry for wrongdoing
	Shows frequent changes of temper
	Trick to get attention
	Almost unconscious unthinking state
	Knowing everything
	Study of religious ideas and beliefs
	Line of rulers from the same family
	Belief based on old ideas of magic/luck
	Cruel unjust ruler
	Avoid
	Bad person
	Say in another way with same meaning

adequate   dynasty   eponymous   eschew
fetters   gimmick   omniscient   paradox
paraphrase   periphery   perplex   plausible
reinforce   repent   stupor   superstition
temperamental   theology   tyrant   upheaval   villain

Exercise

Put the new words into the gaps in the correct grammatical form:

1) There were _____ supplies of food for the voyage.

2) The castle was _____ with strong ramparts.

3) There is a _____ that says if you break a mirror, you get seven years' bad luck.

4) The bank was offering _____ such as a ball point pen or sticker to attract customers.

5) The fugitive's escape was hampered by the cast iron _____ attached to his leg.

6) The Romanov _____ ruled Russia for many years.

7) The accountant's jargon made her _____.

8) Students cannot just copy the exact words from books; they need to _____ what they have read.

9) Hampton is a prosperous suburb on the _____ of London.

10) As she was on a diet, she _____ all high-calorie food such as chocolates.

11) Oliver Twist is the _____ hero of the novel by Charles Dickens.

12) To become a priest you need to study _____.

13) Martin came back from the ale house in a drunken _____ and crashed out on his sofa.

14) Moving home can be a great _____ in your life.

15) He was so _____, you never knew what mood he would be in.

Useful Vocabulary 19

Match the words with their definitions:

	Wood for building
	Metal on padlock fastening a door
	Embarrassing because of complete failure
	Swelling in or on the body
	Tendon (connecting muscle to bone)
	Determination when doing something hard
	Very cruel act
	Hospital
	Expression used so often it lost its meaning
	Cause of trouble
	'ing' form of a verb used as a noun
	Extremely upset from suffering
	Decorate/add beauty
	Express great pleasure of own success
	Give
	Clothed/covered
	Sudden violent attack
	Long dispute between two people/groups
	Attempt to do something new or difficult
	Completely surround/cover
	Very powerful attack

abscess   adorn   assault   atrocity
bane   bestow   clad   cliché
endeavour   engulf   feud   gerund
gloat   harrowing   hasp   ignominious
infirmary   mettle   onslaught   sinew   timber

Exercise

Put the new words into the gaps in the correct grammatical form:

1) On the banks of the Thames, the buildings were _____ with classical features.

2) A tsunami _____ the Japanese city of Ishinomaki.

3) After years of toiling in the factory he had _____ all over his limbs.

4) "A game of two halves" is a classic football _____.

5) He damaged his _____ training with dumbbells in the gym.

6) When you want to make a verb the subject of the sentence you use a _____.

7) The king _____ a great fortune to his heirs.

8) His illegible handwriting was the _____ of the teacher's life.

9) In Romeo and Juliet the Montagues and the Capulets were engaged in a bitter _____.

10) Susan had a boating accident and ended up at the _____.

11) They cut down trees and used the _____ to build a galleon to sail on the high seas.

12) After winning the race, Ralph turned to his rivals and _____.

13) The building was _____ with plastic panels.

14) The intruder broke off the _____ of the locked gate in order to gain entry.

15) Captain Scott relied on his _____ when attempting to reach the South Pole.

Useful Vocabulary 20

Match the words with their definitions:

	Peaceful and calm
	Pour liquid from one container to another
	Action causing public shock/outrage
	Too serious and trying to be important
	Make fun of (often copying) in an unkind way
	Man dressed in expensive, fashionable clothes
	Unimportant and not worth paying attention to
	Not strict
	Do something to show you have power
	Large important city
	Laugh loudly at something stupid
	Tell the truth even when uncomfortable
	Enter where you are not welcome/expected
	Ask many questions to get information
	Substance for cleaning that kills bacteria
	Examine carefully to get the truth
	Unpreventable from happening
	Strong disagreement about a plan
	Agreement to marry someone
	Criticize for not being good enough
	Punish for doing something bad to you

```
assert      dandy        decant       disinfectant
dissent     engagement   frank        guffaw
inevitable  interrogate  intrude      investigate
lenient     mock         metropolis   petty
portentous  reprisal     reproach     scandal     tranquil
```

Exercise

Put the new words into the gaps in the correct grammatical form:

1) She liked to stroll by the river as it was very _____.

2) He _____ the port from the bottle to an elaborate glass decanter.

3) The police _____ the man for many hours before he confessed to his heinous crime.

4) They used _____ to maintain hygiene standards in the infirmary.

5) He was a _____ teacher and everyone liked him.

6) Not being one to beat about the bush, he gave him some _____ advice.

7) He was a _____ criminal, pilfering small things from shops.

8) Playing poker for high stakes every night, it was _____ that it would all end in tears.

9) Charles looked rather _____ in his three piece new suit.

10) The detective _____ the homicide.

11) Hong Kong is a great example of a _____.

12) The revelation of corruption allegations caused a great _____.

13) The family gathered to celebrate the _____ of the couple.

14) As food rations began to diminish, _____ began to rise in the country.

15) With the enemy approaching, they feared fierce _____.

63

Review 5 *(use the vocabulary from 17 - 20)*

Across
4. attack
5. give
6. stick out
9. hospital
12. edge
15. come from
16. steal
17. laugh

Down
1. city
2. main idea
3. avoid
4. very cruel act
6. confuse
7. wood
8. special language
10. tease
11. honest
12. unimportant
13. say another way
14. say sorry

Phobias

Fear of water	
Fear of flying	
Fear of machines	
Fear of light	
Fear of time	
Fear of open spaces	
Fear of anything new	
Fear of fire	
Fear of large things	
Fear of noise	
Fear of small things	
Fear of many things	
Fear of meat	
Fear of England/English culture	
Fear of people	
Fear of books	
Fear of the night	
Fear of spiders	
Fear of crowds	
Fear of horses	
Fear of injury	

Acousticophobia   Agoraphobia   Anglophobia   Anthrophobia
Arachnephobia   Arsonphobia   Aviophobia   Bibliophobia
Carnophobia   Chronophobia   Demophobia   Equinophobia
Hydrophobia   Mechanophobia   Megalophobia   Microphobia
Neophobia   Noctiphobia   Photophobia   Polyphobia
Traumatophobia

Answer Key

Adjectives 1-4 (P2-9)

Adjectives 1	Adjectives 2	Adjectives 3	Adjectives 4
Affluent	Hapless	Sacred	Scenic
Dignified	Fickle	Negligent	Torrid
Choppy	Isolated	Perpetual	Saggy
Ambiguous	Eligible	Optimistic	Torrential
Candid	Inhabited	Reliant	Unilateral
Boggy	Fatal	Malformed	Seditious
Aggressive	Hostile	Repugnant	Unconventional
Compulsive	Loyal	Painstaking	Tertiary
Blazing	Excessive	Materialistic	Vigilant
Elementary	Legitimate	Quick-tempered	Tentative
Affable	Honourable	Pathetic	Well-heeled
Diligent	Judicious	Miffed	Sedentary
Bumbling	Enticing	Relevant	Unassailable
Detrimental	Lucid	Odious	Wondrous
Eerie	Intrepid	Restless	Woeful
1 eerie	1 fatal	1 restless	1 scenic
2 aggressive	2 intrepid	2 perpetual	2 unconventional
3 affluent	3 excessive	3 quick-tempered	3 unassailable
4 choppy	4 lucid	4 malformed	4 well-heeled
5 diligent	5 hapless	5 reliant	5 wondrous
6 elementary	6 inhabited	6 optimistic	6 sedentary
7 dignified	7 isolated	7 materialistic	7 vigilant
8 detrimental	8 enticing	8 odious	8 torrential
9 blazing	9 eligible	9 sacred	9 tentative
10 bumbling	10 fickle	10 negligent	10 tertiary
11 candid	11 hostile	11 painstaking	11 woeful
12 ambiguous	12 loyal	12 relevant	12 torrid

Adjective Exercises 1 and 2 (p10-11)

Various combinations

Adverbs 1-3 (p12-17)

Adverbs 1	Adverbs 2	Adverbs 3
Immeasurably	Kiddingly	Righteously
Evocatively	Mortally	Valiantly
Diabolically	Majestically	Reproachfully
Financially	Potentially	Primly
Coaxingly	Lithely	Sporadically
Ethically	Perpetually	Sheepishly
Abnormally	Kookily	Vivaciously
Intermittently	Offensively	Reassuringly
Constantly	Methodically	Unabashedly
Intently	Outrageously	Puzzlingly
Customarily	Irascibly	Singularly
Assuredly	Menacingly	Seditiously
Frenetically	Paradoxically	Quizzically
Formerly	Irrefutably	Unilaterally

Bleakly	Persistently	Spasmodically
1 financially	1 majestically	1 valiantly
2 formerly	2 perpetually	2 seditiously
3 assuredly	3 kiddingly	3 unabashedly
4 abnormally	4 mortally	4 sheepishly
5 intensely	5 outrageously	5 primly
6 consistently	6 menacingly	6 sporadically
7 diabolically	7 paradoxically	7 quizzically
8 bleakly	8 methodically	8 puzzlingly
9 coaxingly	9 offensively	9 reassuringly
10 intermittently	10 persistently	10 unilaterally
11 customarily	11 potentially	11 reproachfully
12 frenetically	12 irrefutably	12 vivaciously

Adverb Exercises 1 and 2 (p18-19)

Various combinations

Useful Vocabulary 1-5 (p20-30)

Useful Vocabulary 1	Useful Vocabulary 2	Useful Vocabulary 3	Useful Vocabulary 4	Useful Vocabulary 5
Bespoke	Aroma	Sodden	Tempest	Hefty
Flatter	Apprentice	Brandish	Chomp	Dominate
Gem	Boulder	Captive	Fastidious	Brood
Pummel	Congregate	Embolden	Decoy	Gaffe
Assassinate	Enterprise	Incline	Ample	Omit
Hesitate	Impregnable	Adulation	Infamous	Import
Eloquent	Ponder	Retrieve	Glee	Busk
Ventilate	Conundrum	Sheer	Pandemonium	Scrutinize
Complacent	Commotion	Ancestor	Bazaar	Entice
Punitive	Murky	Ornate	Stallion	Swot
Controversy	Implicit	Brawl	Browse	Fiend
Fluctuate	Unscrupulous	Bridle	Disembark	Gust
Flee	Abominable	Curt	Snag	Capacity
Slogan	Vociferous	Vertigo	Carnivore	Auditorium
Impromptu	Phobia	Uncanny	Inherit	Sceptic
Commemorate	Tolerant	Dormant	Erode	Tacit
Penetrate	Plateau	Trivial	Juvenile	Accumulate
Tentatively	Spontaneous	Contempt	Tabloid	Mortgage
Dismay	Ajar	Tendon	Empathy	Labour
Rupture	Plead	Inhabitant	Antics	Merit
Ruse	Liberate	Excruciating	Fad	Nether
1 penetrate	1 boulder	1 vertigo	1 tempest	1 mortgage
2 fluctuates	2 ajar	2 inhabitants	2 ample	2 accumulated
3 eloquent	3 impregnable	3 adulation	3 disembarked	3 omit
4 assassinated	4 pleading	4 ornate	4 browsed	4 scrutinized
5 fled	5 apprentice	5 brandished	5 glee	5 swot
6 hesitated	6 liberated	6 incline	6 carnivores	6 auditorium
7 bespoke	7 murky	7 contempt	7 juveniles	7 gaffe
8 slogan	8 phobia	8 excruciating	8 chomped	8 hefty
9 impromptu	9 aroma	9 ancestors	9 fastidious	9 imports
10 ruptured	10 vociferous	10 sodden	10 inherited	10 brood
11 commemorated	11 congregated	11 bridle	11 erode	11 dominated
12 gem	12 spontaneous	12 tendons	12 empathy	12 gust
13 ruse	13 conundrum	13 brawl	13 fad	13 busking

| 14 tentatively | 14 tolerant | 14 captive | 14 bazaar | 14 capacity |
| 15 ventilate | 15 pondered | 15 dormant | 15 tabloid | 15 labour |

Useful Vocabulary 6-10 (p31-41)

Useful Vocabulary 6	Useful Vocabulary 7	Useful Vocabulary 8	Useful Vocabulary 9	Useful Vocabulary 10
Marine	Capitalism	Panorama	Amble	Gorge
Apprehend	Fauna	Bandit	Garment	Empathize
Fluke	Machete	Lout	Deputy	Juxtapose
Endorse	Deduct	Hindsight	Hybrid	Deity
Larder	Recede	Defy	Lashings	Mainstream
Budget	Mandible	Gild	Carcass	Notion
Bedazzle	Offspring	Elite	Confiscate	Adage
Hoard	Neglect	Novice	Scoff	Likelihood
Gastronomy	Acquire	Knick-knacks	Emancipate	Kerfuffle
Oath	Saunter	Manhandle	Faux pas	Sabre
Applause	Pedlar	Saga	Hanker	Barricade
Cannibal	Plethora	Banter	Assail	Halcyon
Diplomacy	Gentry	Opine	Oblivion	Innate
Ravage	Thrice	Brink	Beckon	Odyssey
Induce	Hermit	Flora	Matriarchy	Altercation
Corrode	Emerge	Languor	Lest	Therapy
Nausea	Bastion	Anarchy	Redolent	Void
Paraphernalia	Lacerate	Carnage	Brawn	Calibre
Decadent	Impartial	Ignite	Kindred	Fable
Saturate	Lieutenant	Relic	Improper	Reap
Jabber	Quibble	Citadel	Patter	Pact
1 ravaged	1 sauntered	1 panorama	1 redolent	1 gorge
2 apprehended	2 impartial	2 flora	2 pattered	2 halcyon
3 hoarded	3 fauna	3 bandits	3 faux pas	3 calibre
4 decadent	4 lieutenant	4 citadel	4 ambled	4 odyssey
5 applause	5 deducted	5 elite	5 improper	5 fables
6 fluke	6 neglected	6 anarchy	6 deputy	6 adage
7 budget	7 capitalism	7 banter	7 hankered	7 sabre
8 bedazzled	8 receded	8 knick-knacks	8 beckoned	8 empathize
9 oath	9 machete	9 ignited	9 oblivion	9 pact
10 corroded	10 inherited	10 louts	10 confiscate	10 void
11 diplomacy	11 plethora	11 manhandled	11 emancipate	11 altercation
12 endorsed	12 emerged	12 brink	12 hybrid	12 barricades
13 cannibals	13 offspring	13 relics	13 carcass	13 reaped
14 larder	14 hermit	14 carnage	14 garments	14 innate
15 nausea	15 quibbled	15 sagas	15 lashings	15 therapy

Useful Vocabulary 11-15 (p42-52)

Useful Vocabulary 11	Useful Vocabulary 12	Useful Vocabulary 13	Useful Vocabulary 14	Useful Vocabulary 15
Solace	Terrain	Jetty	Gully	Furrow
Tirade	Splurge	Abode	Shroud	Eccentric
Squander	Serene	Digit	Grime	Pulse
Connoisseur	Scourge	Enmity	Shatter	Countenance
Perspective	Profligate	Speculate	Stubble	Poise
Dire	Devoid	Heave	Surge	Batter

Veteran	Tauten	Enrage	Talon	Scalp
Forage	Haughty	Plunge	Brambles	Gasp
Vex	Rectitude	Loiter	Downpour	Grimace
Concession	Doctrine	Motif	Cascade	Crease
Reverent	Tacky	Aromatic	Scald	Hamper
Myopic	Frivolous	Clamber	Draught	Anticipate
Unanimous	Sojourn	Plump	Belch	Tramp
Undulate	Aberration	Envelop	Vivid	Numb
Amenity	Umbrage	Stupendous	Cauldron	Lear
Seldom	Irk	Officious	Prowl	Coil
Mortified	Clergy	Multitude	Lichen	Trance
Pledge	Prospect	Errant	Gnaw	Demeanour
Intimate	Erratic	Specious	Canopy	Sneer
Initial	Curb	Quota	Dart	Gash
Viscous	Traipse	Tinder	Majestic	Sinister
1 concession	1 splurged	1 plunged	1 lichen	1 eccentric
2 mortified	2 irked	2 plump	2 downpour	2 anticipating
3 amenities	3 terrain	3 enveloped	3 belched	3 hampered
4 perspective	4 traipse	4 jetty	4 darted	4 gasped
5 connoisseur	5 tacky	5 aromatic	5 brambles	5 battered
6 myopic	6 umbrage	6 abode	6 prowling	6 numb
7 squandered	7 clergy	7 clambered	7 cascaded	7 crease
8 unanimous	8 profligate	8 loitering	8 talon	8 trance
9 undulated	9 prospect	9 enraged	9 draught	9 furrows
10 foraged	10 devoid	10 tinder	10 shroud	10 grimaced
11 pledged	11 sojourned	11 heave	11 scalded	11 gash
12 dire	12 serene	12 quota	12 gnaw	12 pulse
13 intimate	13 erratic	13 stupendous	13 shattered	13 scalp
14 veteran	14 tauten	14 officious	14 stubble	14 sinister
15 solace	15 scourge	15 speculate	15 vivid	15 tramps

Useful Vocabulary 16-20 (p53-63)

Useful Vocabulary 16	Useful Vocabulary 17	Useful Vocabulary 18	Useful Vocabulary 19	Useful Vocabulary 20
Hobble	Protrude	Periphery	Timber	Tranquil
Emaciated	Gunge	Plausible	Hasp	Decant
Meek	Brutal	Reinforce	Ignominious	Scandal
Forlorn	Pagan	Paradox	Abscess	Portentous
Reek	Hyperbole	Upheaval	Sinew	Mock
Furtive	Jargon	Perplex	Mettle	Dandy
Tic	Havoc	Fetters	Atrocity	Petty
Ooze	Pompous	Eponymous	Infirmary	Lenient
Crumple	Potpourri	Adequate	Cliché	Assert
Bulbous	Manifesto	Repent	Bane	Metropolis
Scorn	Skim	Temperamental	Gerund	Guffaw
Contort	Allure	Gimmick	Harrowing	Frank
Tuft	Pilfer	Stupor	Adorn	Intrude
Manic	Flabby	Omniscient	Gloat	Interrogate
Barb	Peruse	Theology	Bestow	Disinfectant
Tussock	Curriculum	Dynasty	Clad	Investigate
Singe	Sullen	Superstition	Assault	Inevitable
Bile	Gist	Tyrant	Feud	Dissent
Slobber	Wreak	Eschew	Endeavour	Engagement
Scuttle	Emanate	Villain	Engulf	Reproach

Temples	Stark	Paraphrase	Onslaught	Reprisal
1 hobbled	1 potpourri	1 adequate	1 adorned	1 tranquil
2 bulbous	2 pilfer	2 reinforced	2 engulfed	2 decanted
3 bile	3 allure	3 superstition	3 abscesses	3 interrogated
4 meek	4 gist	4 gimmicks	4 cliché	4 disinfectant
5 contorted	5 jargon	5 fetters	5 sinew	5 lenient
6 scuttle	6 curriculum	6 dynasty	6 gerund	6 frank
7 forlorn	7 gunge	7 perplexed	7 bestowed	7 petty
8 singed	8 manifesto	8 paraphrase	8 bane	8 inevitable
9 crumpled	9 emanating	9 periphery	9 feud	9 dandy
10 tuft	10 skimmed	10 eschewed	10 infirmary	10 investigated
11 barbs	11 oozed	11 eponymous	11 timber	11 metropolis
12 emaciated	12 flabby	12 theology	12 gloated	12 scandal
13 oozed	13 havoc	13 stupor	13 clad	13 engagement
14 temples	14 stark	14 upheaval	14 hasp	14 dissent
15 reeked	15 sullen	15 temperamental	15 mettle	15 reprisals

Phobias (p65)

Hydrophobia; Aviophobia; Mechanophobia; Photophobia; Chronophobia; Agoraphobia; Neophobia; Arsonphobia; Megalophobia; Acouticophobia; Microphobia; Polyphobia; Carnophobia; Anglophobia; Anthrophobia; Bibliophobia; Noctiphobia; Arachnephobia; Demophobia; Equinophobia; Traumatophobia

Printed in Great Britain
by Amazon